PLAN A
LIFE
YOU LOVE
& LIVE IT OUT LOUD NOW
JOURNAL

I0458735

A BOLD CONTINUATION OF THE
JOURNEY THAT TRANSFORMED LIVES

HANNA OLIVAS
ALONG WITH 6 INSPIRING AUTHORS

Table of Contents

Hanna Olivas

Founder and CEO of SHE RISES STUDIOS

https://www.linkedin.com/company/she-rises-studios/
https://www.facebook.com/sherisesstudios
https://www.instagram.com/sherisesstudios_llc/
www.SheRisesStudios.com

Author, Speaker, and Founder. Hanna was born and raised in Las Vegas, Nevada, and has paved her way to becoming one of the most influential women of 2022. Hanna is the co-founder of She Rises Studios and the founder of the Brave & Beautiful Blood Cancer Foundation. Her journey started in 2017 when she was first diagnosed with Multiple Myeloma, an incurable blood cancer. Now more than ever, her focus is to empower other women to become leaders because The Future is Female. She is currently traveling and speaking publicly to women to educate them on entrepreneurship, leadership, and owning the female power within.

Plan A Life You Love & Live It Out Loud Now: The Journal

A Movement · A Manifesto · A Mirror · A Memoir · A Legacy

Dear Woman on the Journey,

This journal is more than blank pages. It's a mirror to see yourself clearly, a manifesto to claim what you believe, and a movement to live boldly and unapologetically.

Inside these pages, you'll find space to:

- Reflect on your story with gut-honest honesty.
- Dream of what's possible with courage.
- Take practical steps to build a life that fits you—not anyone else's version of you.
- Write the legacy you want to leave behind.

You're not just filling in prompts. You're writing the story of your life—out loud, on purpose, and with love.

With you on the journey,

Hanna Olivas, The Resilience Maven™ | Author, Mother, Fighter, Creator of Sheconomy™

Part 1: The Mirror – Seeing Yourself Clearly

Honesty is the first step to freedom.

- **How well am I sleeping, and how does it impact my daily life?**
- **What is my relationship with food and exercise, and how does it affect my energy levels?**
- **Are my physical needs being met? Am I taking the time for self-care activities?**
- **Write down 3 simple things you can do to improve your health right now, and implement them into your day moving forward.**

Exercise: Draw two columns: "The life I'm living" vs. "The life I desire." Circle the differences that matter most.

"The first step toward change is awareness."
– Nathaniel Branden

"The first step toward change is awareness."
– Nathaniel Branden

Part 2: The Awakening – Remembering Who You Are

Before you plan, you must remember your worth.

- **What makes me feel most like myself?**
- **What gifts have I been hiding?**
- **Where in my life do I feel God (or my higher self) affirming me?**
- **When was the last time I felt proud of myself?**

Exercise: Write a "Who I Am" list—at least 20 words or phrases that describe your true identity, not your roles.

"You are not behind. You are becoming."

"You are not behind. You are becoming."

Part 3: The Movement – Dreaming Boldly

Permission granted. Dream wide, dream deep, dream loud.

- **If nothing was impossible, what would I try?**
- **What dreams have I buried because they felt "too much"?**
- **What would I do differently if I trusted provision would come?**

Exercise: Close your eyes and visualize your best life 5 years from now. Write it out in detail.

"Don't shrink your dreams. Stretch your courage."

"Don't shrink your dreams. Stretch your courage."

Part 4: The Manifesto – Living with Intention

This is where you decide, declare, and design your life.

- **What 3 values will guide my choices from here on out?**
- **Where do I need to be braver in my "yes" and firmer in my "no"?**
- **What limiting belief will I rewrite today?**

Exercise: Write your **Personal Manifesto**: one page declaring who you are and how you choose to live out loud.

"Clarity is the mother of courage."

"Clarity is the mother of courage."

Part 5: The Healing – From Breakdowns to Breakthroughs

Your pain is part of your power.

- **What wound am I still carrying that needs attention?**
- **What patterns do I see in my breakdown moments?**
- **Where do I need to show myself compassion?**

Exercise: Write a Release Letter to someone or something you need to let go of.

"Out of difficulties grow miracles."
– Jean de La Bruyère

"Out of difficulties grow miracles."
– Jean de La Bruyère

Part 6: The Memoir – Owning Your Story

Every chapter matters—even the messy ones.

- **What's the hardest thing I've overcome?**
- **What chapter of my story am I most proud of?**
- **What "failure" became a blessing in disguise?**

Exercise: Write a short story of a time you overcame something you thought you couldn't.

"Your story is the key that can unlock someone else's prison."

"Your story is the key that can unlock
someone else's prison."

Part 7: The Legacy – Writing What Lasts

Your life is your message. What do you want it to say?

- **What do I want to be remembered for?**
- **What wisdom do I want to pass down?**
- **Who do I want to impact with my story?**

Exercise: Write a Letter to Your Future Self, 10 years from now.

"Carve your name on hearts, not tombstones."
– Shannon Alder

"Carve your name on hearts, not tombstones."
– **Shannon Alder**

Part 8: The Celebration – Living It Out Loud Now

Don't wait until later—celebrate now.

- **What wins (big or small) can I celebrate today?**
- **What brave action have I already taken?**
- **How can I bring more joy into my life now?**

Exercise: Create a Joy List—25 things that make you smile..

"Joy is not in things; it is in us."
– **Richard Wagner**

"Joy is not in things; it is in us."
– **Richard Wagner**

Part 9: The Connection – Building Your Circle

We don't do life alone. Find your people, fuel your purpose.

- **Who truly supports my dreams?**
- **What relationships drain me instead of fill me?**
- **Who do I need to forgive or release?**
- **Who inspires me to live more boldly?**

Exercise: Draw your Circle of Support. In the center, write your name. Around it, write names of those who uplift and inspire you..

"Surround yourself with those who see your light and remind you of it."

"Surround yourself with those who see your light and
remind you of it."

Part 10: The Daily Practice – Living Out Loud Everyday

Legacies aren't built in one moment—they're built daily.

- **What 3 daily practices help me stay aligned?**
- **How will I start my mornings with intention?**
- **What ritual will I end my evenings with?**
- **How can I check in with myself weekly?**

Exercise: Create a Daily Out Loud Ritual—a morning or evening practice that keeps you grounded (could be journaling, prayer, gratitude, affirmations, or breathwork)..

What you do every day matters more than what you do once in a while."

"Carve your name on hearts, not tombstones."
– **Shannon Alder**

Affirmations for Living Out Loud

- I am free to design a life that feels like home.
- My voice, my story, and my presence matter.
- I don't need permission to shine.
- I am building my legacy today.

Legacy Declaration Page

"I choose to stop waiting and start living. I choose to live out loud. I commit to building a life I love—boldly, bravely, and beautifully. This is my legacy."

_____

Signature / Date

Gabby Gutierrez

The beauty of success by Gabby G
Inspirational,motivational life and business coach
and a Brand Ambassador

http://www.linkedin.com/in/gabby-gutierrez-b16ab736
https://www.facebook.com/gabby.gutierrez.9081
https://www.instagram.com/gabbygu9/
https://thebeautyofsuccess.com/

Gabby Gutierrez is a passionate and determined woman who has devoted her life to helping others discover their purpose, embrace their potential, and create lives filled with joy and fulfillment. With over 30 years of experience as a successful entrepreneur, Gabby has influenced and inspired thousands of women worldwide, guiding them to rise above challenges and step boldly into their own power.

As one of the top leaders in the company she represents, Gabby has proven that resilience, dedication, and heart-driven leadership can transform not only businesses but also lives. Her journey has been shaped by personal experiences that she now channels into empowering others—turning every lesson into an opportunity to serve, uplift, and guide.

Fueled by an unwavering passion for personal cevelopment, Gabby is constantly exploring new ways to support and inspire those around her. Whether through her writing, mentorship, or leadership, her mission remains clear: to help people unlock their fullest potential and live happier, more purposeful lives.

Shattered Dreams, Stronger Beginnings: A Companion to Your Journey of Faith and Resilience

This space was created for hearts that have been broken, for dreams that felt lost, and for the quiet hope that still flickers within you.

Life has moments that shatter us. But with God, every ending can be the seed of a new beginning. As you move through these pages, you'll be guided by Scripture, reflection prompts, and prayer invitations to help you process your pain, rediscover your strength, and realign with God's promises.

This is not about rushing your healing or forcing answers. It's about giving yourself permission to be honest, to wrestle, to grieve, and to hope again. Here, your tears are welcome. Your questions are safe. Your faith—no matter how fragile—is enough.

Take your time. Write freely. Let these pages become a sacred space where God meets you, restores you, and whispers: "Your story is not over. I am making all things new."

Welcome to your journey of faith and resilience.

1. The Shattetring Moment

- Think back to a moment in your life when everything changed. What happened?
- How did it make you feel — physically, emotionally, spiritually?
- Write down the raw emotions you felt. Don't edit yourself.

Psalm 34:18 – "The Lord is close to the brokenhearted and saves those who are crushed in spirit."

Psalm 34:18 – "The Lord is close to the brokenhearted
and saves those who are crushed in spirit."

2. Living in the Aftermath

- **What responsibilities kept you going when you felt like giving up?**
- **Who or what did you hide your pain from? Why?**
- **Write a prayer asking God to give you strength for today.**

Corinthians 12:9 – "My grace is sufficient for you, for my power is made perfect in weakness."

Corinthians 12:9 – "My grace is sufficient for you, for
my power is made perfect in weakness."

3. Wrestling with God

- What hard questions have you asked God in your storm?
- Write a letter to God sharing your anger, doubts, or fears.
- What small ways has He reminded you of His presence (songs, people, verses)?

Job 23:3 – "If only I knew where to find Him; if only I could go to His dwelling!"

Job 23:3 – "If only I knew where to find Him; if only I could go to His dwelling!"

4. One Day at a Time

- What feels overwhelming to you right now?
- What's one small step you can take today?
- List three things you're grateful for today, no matter how small.

Matthew 6:34 – "Do not worry about tomorrow... each day has enough trouble of its own."

Matthew 6:34 – "Do not worry about tomorrow... each day has enough trouble of its own."

5. Rebuilding Myself

- Who are you beyond your roles (spouse, parent, leader, etc.)?
- Write down 5 qualities or strengths that make you unique.
- What new beginnings or dreams do you feel God is inviting you into?

Isaiah 61:3 – "...to bestow on them a crown of beauty instead of ashes."

Isaiah 61:3 – "...to bestow on them a crown of beauty instead of ashes."

6. The Power of Faith and Resilience

- Where can you see God already using your pain for good?
- Write about a time when faith carried you further than your strength.
- What does resilience mean to you now?

Romans 8:28 – "In all things God works for the good of those who love him."

Romans 8:28 – "In all things God works for the good of those who love him."

7. A New Beginning

- **What dreams did you think were gone that God might be bringing back?**
- **Describe what your "new chapter" looks like.**
- **Finish this sentence: "With God, my future looks like _____"**

Jeremiah 29:11 – "For I know the plans I have for you... plans to give you hope and a future."

Jeremiah 29:11 – "For I know the plans I have for you...
plans to give you hope and a future."

8. A Word for You

- **If you could encourage someone else going through heartbreak, what would you say?**
- **Write a prayer of blessing over your future self.**
- **Write down one declaration of faith you will hold onto this week (e.g.: I am not alone, My story isn't over.).**

Romans 15:13 – "May the God of hope fill you with all joy and peace as you trust in him…"

Romans 15:13 – "May the God of hope fill you with all
joy and peace as you trust in him…"

Carmen Maendel

Co-CEO of Nate's Property Maintenance LLC

https://www.linkedin.com/in/carmen-maendel-17510944/
https://www.facebook.com/ncmaendel
https://www.instagram.com/maendelcarmen/
https://natespropertymaintenance.com
https://courageouswoman.net

Hello I'm Carmen Maendel. Nate and I are a husband and wife team. Our fifteen year old son, Josh officially works for our company as well. We have embarked upon an entrepreneurial journey together that is extremely rewarding for all of us. We own and operate Nate's Property Maintenance LLC together. I handle the business on the home front while my husband coordinates our projects on the job sites with our clients and team of workers. We compliment each other very well working together, and remain very service oriented in our company. Some of the business roles I perform are the following: balancing our books, regularly posting to social media, scheduling our clients, arranging purchase contracts for new business equipment, keeping our business licenses and registration up to date, documenting client files, and much more. Nate works with our clients by coordinating all the projects and equipment on the job sites and carefully plans for each of our projects we do down to the finest of details.

Windows into My Soul Journal

Your life has many layers — body, mind, heart, spirit, and community — and each tells part of your story. This journal invites you to pause and look through nine windows of health: Physical, Emotional, Intellectual, Social, Spiritual, Financial, Environmental, Occupational, and Cultural.

Each section offers guiding questions, Scripture, and simple steps to help you reflect honestly, care for your whole self, and invite God into every area of your life. This is not about perfection, but progress — opening space for healing, growth, and renewal.

May these pages be your safe place to listen, reflect, and allow God's light to shine through every window of your soul.

Window #1: Physical Health

- How well am I sleeping, and how does it impact my daily life?
- What is my relationship with food and exercise, and how does it affect my energy levels?
- Are my physical needs being met? Am I taking the time for self-care activities?
- Write down 3 simple things you can do to improve your health right now, and implement them into your day moving forward.

Carmen Macadel Photography

Jeremiah 17:14
"Heal me, O Lord, and I shall be healed; save me, and I shall be saved, for you are my praise."

Jeremiah 17:14
"Heal me, O Lord, and I shall be healed; save me, and I
shall be saved, for you are my praise."

Window #2: Emotional Health

- **What emotions am I experiencing most often, and why?**
- **How do I typically respond to stress and pressure, and what does that reveal about my coping mechanisms?**
- **What needs of mine are not being met, and how can I address them?**
- **Write down how you feel emotionally 3 times a day for 1 week (am, noon, pm), and notice how you feel at different times of the day.**

Carmen Maendel Photography

Psalm 34:18
"The Lord is close to the brokenhearted and saves those who are crushed in spirit."

Psalm 34:18
"The Lord is close to the brokenhearted and saves those
who are crushed in spirit."

Window #3: Intellectual Health

- Is curiosity and a love of learning cultivated daily in my life?
- Are critical and creative thinking skills used, or are information and ideas passively accepted by me?
- Is there space for reflection and intellectual integration, and are knowledge and skills applied in meaningful ways?
- Brainstorm for 10 minutes about how you think your life could improve overall and implement these ideas into your life.

Carmen Maendel Photography

Romans 12:2

"Do not conform to the pattern of this world, but be transformed by the renewing of your mind. Then you will be able to test and approve what God's will is—his good, pleasing and perfect will."

Romans 12:2
"Do not conform to the pattern of this world, but be transformed by the renewing of your mind. Then you will be able to test and approve what God's will is—his good, pleasing and perfect will."

Window #4: Social Health

- Who are the people I regularly connect with, and how do those relationships contribute to my overall happiness and well-being?
- Do I feel supported and understood in my social interactions, and do I offer the same to others?
- Am I making a positive impact on the communities I'm a part of? Do I feel a sense of belonging?
- Call up a friend/s of yours and meet them for coffee, and write down how you felt after you met with them.

Mark 12:31
"The second is this: 'Love your neighbor as yourself.'
There is no other commandment greater than these."

Mark 12:31
"The second is this: 'Love your neighbor as yourself.'
There is no other commandment greater than these."

Window #5: Spiritual Health

- **Is my life in alignment with spiritual principles? If not, what changes can be made?**
- **How do I define spirituality and what experiences have shaped my spiritual beliefs and practices?**
- **How are challenges and setbacks handled in a way that aligns with my spiritual beliefs?**
- **Find one Bible verse that you can relate to and stand upon, and recite it 3 times in the am and the pm for 1 month.**

Carmen Macnaa Photography

Isaiah 40:31

"But those who hope in the Lord will renew their strength. They will soar on wings like eagles; they will run and not grow weary, they will walk and not faint."

Isaiah 40:31
"But those who hope in the Lord will renew their
strength. They will soar on wings like eagles; they will
run and not grow weary, they will walk and not faint."

Window 6: Financial Health

- **What does "financial security" truly mean to me, and are my actions aligned with that definition?**
- **How do my past experiences and beliefs about money impact my current financial decisions and habits?**
- **If money were no object, how would I truly live, and how can I start incorporating elements of that life into present circumstances, aligned with my values?**
- **Write down your experience with money growing up, and your attitude toward money today.**

Luke 6:38
"Give, and it will be given to you. A good measure, pressed down, shaken together, and running over, will be poured into your lap. For with the measure you use, it will be measured back to you."

Luke 6:38
"Give, and it will be given to you. A good measure,
pressed down, shaken together, and running over, will
be poured into your lap. For with the measure you use,
it will be measured back to you."

Window 7: Environmental Health

- How does my physical environment impact my health and happiness?
- Am I connected to and respectful of the natural world?
- How do my daily habits contribute to or detract from environmental health?
- Write down 3 things you can do today to make the world a better place in general, and implement them.

Carmen Maendel Photography

Psalm 24:1
"The earth is the LORD's, and the fullness thereof; the world, and they that dwell therein."

Psalm 24:1
"The earth is the LORD's, and the fullness thereof; the
world, and they that dwell therein."

Window 8: Occupational Health

- Do my values and beliefs align with my current work?, Does it leave me feeling hopeful and authentic, or does it drain me?
- What specific changes in work or in my personal life would truly improve work-life balance and allow me to thrive, and am I actively seeking or implementing those changes?
- Am I truly engaged and motivated in my work, or am I experiencing signs of burnout, such as persistent fatigue, cynicism, or detachment, and how am I addressing these signs?
- Write down your energy level 1-10 for 3 times a day for 1 week (am, noon, pm), and notice the times you have high and low energy.

Carmen Maendel Photography

Mark 2:27

"Then he said to them, 'The Sabbath was made for man, not man for the Sabbath'"

Mark 2:27
"Then he said to them, 'The Sabbath was made for man,
not man for the Sabbath'"

Window 9: Cultural Health

- How do cultural values, beliefs, and practices shape the understanding of my "good health" and "well-being," and are they aligned with how my life is lived?
- In what specific situations or relationships does cultural background, identity, or practices create challenges or opportunities for me for deeper connection and understanding with others?
- How do I cultivate and maintain a sense of belonging and connection within my cultural community, and how does this belonging (or lack thereof) impact my overall sense of self and well-being?
- Initiate, and engage in a conversation with 3 people that you do not know this week, and focus on listening more than talking.

Colossians 3:11
"Here there is no Greek and Jew, circumcision and uncircumcision, barbarian, Scythian, slave, free; but Christ is all and in all."

Colossians 3:11
"Here there is no Greek and Jew, circumcision and
uncircumcision, barbarian, Scythian, slave, free; but
Christ is all and in all."

Colossians 3:11
"Here there is no Greek and Jew, circumcision and
uncircumcision, barbarian, Scythian, slave, free; but
Christ is all and in all."

Erica Elliott

WarriorHeart Healing Hearts
Counselor, Brain Code Strategist, Speaker, and Author

https://www.linkedin.com/in/erica-elliott-ms-lpc-b90911150
https://www.facebook.com/warriorheartxo
https://www.instagram.com/warriorheartxo
https://msha.ke/warriorheartxo
https://linktr.ee/WarriorHeartxo

I possess a Master's Degree in Counseling Psychology and have invested over three decades in my career as a Licensed Counselor, Certified Brain Health Coach, and Certified Health Integrative Medicine Professional. My expertise encompasses a broad spectrum of therapeutic approaches, such as Neurobiology, ADHD and Neurodiversity, Somatic Therapy, Energy Medicine, NLP, CBT, RET, EFT, TFT, Theology, EMDR, the Gottman Method, alongside Mindfulness and Meditation. I am an international acclaimed author, speaker and spent over a decade in the military.I am the owner of WarriorHeart Healing Hearts. As a Brain Code Strategist I champion a comprehensive healing approach to harmonizes the mind, body, and spirit. I help individuals clear up the mess to discover their MASTERPIECE using a combination of healing modalities to rapidly rewire for success!Throughout my career, I've had the privilege of helping thousands of individuals, viewing my work not merely as a profession but as a calling. I am truly passionate about empowering others to grow, heal, and soar, unlocking the incredible life that God has always envisioned for them.Having navigated my own share of trials, traumas, and triggers, I deeply understand that healing flourishes through compassionate relationships. Together, we cultivate resilience and vitality, transforming legacies. Like iron sharpening iron, if you're looking for support or just want to connect, you were destined for greatness! Be Blessed and Be a Blessing!

7-Step Blueprint to a Blessed and Abundant Life

What follows are the 7 steps God walked me through—biblical, neurological, and personal practices that created freedom and clarity from the inside out. These aren't theories. They are lived truths. They're the process of becoming who God designed you to be.

his journal is your guide through 7 biblical and brain-based steps that renew the mind, heal the heart, and realign you with God's best. These are not theories, but lived truths that can shift your life from the inside out.
Take your time. Write honestly. Breathe deeply. Let this be your space to connect with God and step into the blessed and abundant life He designed for you.

"Freedom begins within—the journey of becoming who God designed you to be."

Step 1: Pause and Breathe

From a brain science perspective, breath is powerful. When you breathe deeply and rhythmically, you activate the parasympathetic nervous system—your body's natural rest-and-digest mechanism. It counteracts the fight-or-flight mode that's triggered by stress and trauma. Deep breathing also helps quiet the amygdala, the part of the brain responsible for fear and emotional reactivity, and strengthens activity in the prefrontal cortex, the center for logic, reasoning, and executive decision-making.

Genesis 2:7 says, "Then the Lord God formed a man from the dust of the ground and breathed into his nostrils the breath of life, and the man became a living being." That breath—God's breath—was our origin. And when we pause to breathe with intention, we are reconnecting to the very life force of heaven. It is a moment of realignment, a sacred pause.

Breathing isn't just relaxation—it's neurological reprogramming. When we breathe slowly and intentionally, we send a message to the brain that we are safe. And when the brain feels safe, it opens up to healing.
Breathing isn't a small thing. It's the foundation. It's the way we pause the chaos and invite heaven in. And sometimes, when that's all you can do—it's more than enough to begin your journey to freedom.

"Each breath is a sacred pause—an invitation to release fear, receive peace, and realign with the life-giving breath of God."

Step 1: Pause and Breathe

Exercise: Take a few minutes to clear with the breath every day. You can breathe in God's Love and Light as you say "I Breathe in Peace," then Breathe out saying something like "I breathe out stress, anxiety, or worry." Do this for about three minutes.

Then start with writing down at least 7 things you are grateful for right now. Go deep what you have prayed for or asked for and were given in the few weeks or months. If you are feeling stuck write at least sixteen to engage your brain in not only remembering but also feeling that more blessings are possible.

"Each breath is a sacred pause—an invitation to release fear, receive peace, and realign with the life-giving breath of God."

"Each breath is a sacred pause—an invitation to release fear, receive peace, and realign with the life-giving breath of God."

Step 2: Notice the Program

It's hard to heal what you don't even know is there. I remember one day, after weeks of feeling like I was making no progress, I found myself crying on the couch again. I had been doing "all the right things," but still felt stuck and so angry at my body for failing me. That's when God dropped a gentle truth into my spirit: "You're still running old programs." That phrase hit me like a wave.

So much of what we do, think, feel, and believe is not conscious. It's patterned. It's programmed. It's rehearsed behavior and belief that was wired into us in childhood, trauma, culture, or experience. And until we notice the program, we'll keep repeating it.
Proverbs 23:7 says, "As a man thinks in his heart, so is he." It doesn't say "as a man thinks in his mind." It says heart—because it's not just about surface thoughts. It's about deep belief systems embedded in your emotional and spiritual core.

From a neuroscience perspective, our brains love patterns. The basal ganglia is the area responsible for habits—whether they're healthy or harmful. If your brain is wired for scarcity, survival, fear, or shame, it will keep repeating those thought loops unless they're interrupted.

The Reticular ActivatingSystem (RAS) also plays a role. It filters the information we notice based on what we believe. If you believe you're not enough, your brain will constantly "prove" that to you by filtering out anything that says otherwise.
You don't have to be controlled by old programming. But you do have to see it first. Awareness is the first miracle.

"Awareness is the first miracle—the moment you see the old program, you begin to break free."

Step 2: Notice the Program

Exercise:

- How are you creating some of your own problems by repeating patterns?
- What patterns are you noticing in your life that are not serving you well?
- When did these patterns start?
- Who or where did I learn them?

It's important to let yourself dive deep here to be able to notice areas and change them more easily (Do this in curiosity not judgement or condemnation). It's only when we get clear that we can change the unconscious programming. You can even start with asking yourself — what do I wish I wasn't doing in life? — so you can see the patterns underneath.

"Awareness is the first miracle—the moment you see the old program, you begin to break free."

"Awareness is the first miracle—the moment you see the
old program, you begin to break free."

Step 3: Speak What You Seek

I'll never forget the day I heard myself say, "I'm so tired of being stuck." And instantly, I felt the Holy Spirit say back, "Then stop reinforcing that narrative with your words." Whoa. That one moment shifted everything.

Our words are not just sounds. They're seeds. They plant into our subconscious and into the spiritual realm. They give our minds—and our miracles—directions to follow.

Mark 11:24 says, "Whatever you ask for in prayer, believe that you have received it, and it will be yours." Belief and declaration go hand in hand. You speak, you believe, and you align your life with that truth.

Neurologically, speaking with intention activates the reticular activating system to start filtering your life through the lens of what you declare. It also begins to change your inner self-perception, which creates emotional safety and promotes rewiring of identity over time.

Your voice is a spiritual and neurological weapon. Speak as if it's already done. Because in the kingdom—it is.

"Your words are seeds—plant what you want to see grow."

Step 3: Speak What You Seek

Exercise: Write out clearly what you want. Then ask yourself if you believe you can have these things. On a scale of 0 to 10 (zero equals not at all and ten equals absolutely), if not, there is a block in receiving it. Once you get clear and see the blocks, you can clear them to allow blessings to flow in more easily.

"Your words are seeds—plant what you want to see grow."

"Your words are seeds—plant what you want to see grow."

Step 4: Visualize the Victory

Before I ever stood on stage, wrote a book, built a business, or even walked into healing, I saw it in my mind and felt it in my soul. I would close my eyes, not to escape—but to prepare. I imagined myself whole, vibrant, focused, even joyful. I saw myself helping others. I envisioned rooms filled with love, joy, and light. I pictured freedom—and it became a seed of faith inside me. This is actually a tool I learned when I was a young girl. When I was about 12 or 13, after reading the Bible out of desperation, God led me to read a book called "The Power of Positive thinking" by Norman Vincent Peale. I began using this tool every night with all the things that I wanted to happen in my life. Every one of those things came true except for one, and that one was one of those things that I would say sometimes I thank God for unanswered prayers.

Hebrews 11:1 tells us, "Now faith is the substance of things hoped for, the evidence of things not seen." Visualization is not fantasy. It's the mental rehearsal of God's promises.

God gave Abraham a vision of stars when he had no child. God gave Joseph dreams before any palace. Jesus even endured the cross "for the joy set before Him." Visualization is a faith act.

From a brain science standpoint, when you visualize vividly, the brain engages the same neural circuits as if it's actually happening. The motor cortex, sensory centers, and emotional processors light up. The body begins to "practice" the experience before it ever arrives. This primes your nervous system and rewires your belief system.

See it until you believe it. Then move like it's already yours.

"Faith sees the finish line before the race begins."

Step 4: Visualize the Victory

Exercise: Create a vision board. Make it fun and colorful. Add quotes and Bible Scriptures. Place it somewhere you can see daily. Lots of businesses and successful people use this tool to help them create a blessed life.

"Faith sees the finish line before the race begins."

"Faith sees the finish line before the race begins."

Step 5: Feel It Fully

There's a sacred moment that happens when you stop running from your emotions and finally sit down with them. For me, it happened late one night, in the quiet, no distractions—just the ache in my chest and the truth I couldn't outrun. I had to feel the grief. The fear. The loss. I had to feel it in order to heal it.

Ecclesiastes 3:4 says that there is "a time to weep and a time to laugh, a time to mourn and a time to dance." Also, from from the poem "Two-Headed Calf" by Laura Gilpin she said that "Most of us want to skip the weeping and get to the dancing. But what you bury alive doesn't die—it grows."

The limbic system, especially the amygdala and hippocampus, stores unprocessed emotional memory. If not released, it keeps the nervous system in a chronic stress loop. But when we feel an emotion fully, name it, breathe into it, and bring it before God, we release it—and make space for joy.

Your emotions are not the enemy. They're invitations to healing.

"What you feel fully, you can finally heal."

Step 5: Feel It Fully

Exercise: Allow yourself to first write out any negative emotions and then take a few minutes to feel into where you feel this in your body. Then saying the feeling like this "I allow myself to feel anger, even though I don't want to feel anger," as you breathe love and light into the area. Do each feeling three times and notice how much it relieves the stress from your body.

We can also use emotions as a guidance system. When we tune in and ask if this feels like a thing that we need to do right now, or how we feel about that? You can strengthen your guidance system, even by asking God which direction should I go right now? If your mind comes up with two or three different directions, test them out, and see which one feels right in your spirit.

Remember, the brain is a program, and sometimes we get confused about which direction to take because the brain gives us a lot of different options. Then we become paralyzed with so many options and take no steps forward. Practicing this regularly can help you release the stress, tune in, and find out which way would feel better for you. Before you know it, you'll be using your emotions as the GPS for creating a more abundant, blessed, and healthy life. Journal what each of these exercises was like for you.

"What you feel fully, you can finally heal."

"What you feel fully, you can finally heal."

Step 6: Rewire with Repetition

Rewiring doesn't happen in a weekend. It happens daily. For me, it was declaring a Scripture over my life when I didn't feel it. It was praying when I was tired. It was doing breathwork when my anxiety said "run." Healing came in layers—through repetition.

Romans 12:2 doesn't just say, 'be transformed.' It says how—"by the renewing of your mind." Renewal is ongoing. Daily. Intentional. Plus Faith is active, not passive.

Neuroplasticity is the brain's ability to form new neural pathways. Repetition strengthens those pathways like a trail in the forest. The more you walk it, the clearer it becomes. Eventually, it becomes the default path.

Consistency by repetition creates clarity. And clarity rewires destiny.

"Repetition is the rhythm that rewrites your mind—and your future."

Step 6: Rewire with Repetition

Exercise: Go back to the exercise of what you really want. Then ask yourself what steps am I taking towards each of these areas in my life? If you're not taking steps forward, then you are not moving towards what you really want in your life.

Many people think if we just get clear about what we want, then it will happen, but it's very important to take steps towards what you want. For example, if you want to become an author, you would want to get involved in author communities. If you want to learn to play piano, then you want to check out places that have classes for piano lessons. Write down each of the things that you said you wanted earlier, and beside them write out 2 to 3 action steps that you could take to move towards them.

"Repetition is the rhythm that rewrites your mind—and your future."

"Repetition is the rhythm that rewrites your mind—and your future."

Step 7: Act in Alignment

Selling everything and starting over wasn't just brave—it was obedience. We didn't have a perfect plan. We had a prompting. And every time we said yes, God met us with provision, guidance, and miracles. Alignment is not just what you believe—it's what you "do" in response to belief.

James 2:17 says, "Faith by itself, if it is not accompanied by action, is dead." Action is the exhale of belief.

When you act in alignment with God's truth, the brain receives feedback that says, "This belief is safe and effective." The prefrontal cortex—your decision-making center—builds stronger executive function and confidence when your actions match your values.

Faith is not passive. It's progressive. And the more you act on truth, the more it becomes your new normal.

"Faith comes alive when your steps match your belief."

Step 7: Act in Alignment

Exercise: Get really clear with this exercise in a way where you ask yourself these questions and write them down: How would I act differently if I had these things in my life? Write out who would I need to become in order to have these things in my life. How would I show up in life if I had these things in my life? How would I feel? How would I think? How would I talk?

Then take 7 minutes a day visualizing the things in life you want and enjoy. Get up and move your body. Put some music on, as you see yourself experiencing the goals and life that you desire. The more you practice exercises like this, having fun while you do it, the easier it becomes for you to clear resistance and move towards obtaining the blessed and abundant life you desire.

"Faith comes alive when your steps match your belief."

"Faith comes alive when your steps match your belief."

Sylvia Becker-Hill

Becker-Hill Inc.

https://www.linkedin.com/in/sylviabeckerhill/
https://www.facebook.com/sylvia.beckerhill/
https://www.instagram.com/sylviabeckerhill/
https://becker-hill.com/
https://sylviabecker-hill.com

Sylvia Becker-Hill is a trailblazing Renaissance Woman and the creator of the Neuro Creativity™ framework, where applied neuroscience, somatic coaching, intentional creativity, and energy management converge. Since 1997, she has empowered thousands of executives, women leaders, and entrepreneurs worldwide to break free from outdated paradigms and design lives of impact and joy.In 2002, Sylvia became the first German coach to earn the coveted Professional Certified Coach designation from the International Coach Federation, and in 2023 she was named one of the world's first ten Certified Master Neuroplasticians—a recognition of her expertise in rewiring the brain for lasting transformation. A multiple international bestselling author and seasoned edutainer, she blends science, soul, and artistry into experiences that spark profound personal transformation.Her mission is clear: to help you "FLIP" everything that blocks, hurts, or sabotages you into unquestionable Freedom, unconditional Love, envisioned Identity, and impactful Power.

-FLIP Waiting to Creating-
The Quantum Practice of Gratitude

Welcome.

This journal is not just a container for your thoughts—it's a sanctuary for your sensations, a mirror for your becoming. Here, gratitude isn't a list—it's a living, breathing frequency that starts in your cells.

As you write, draw, doodle, or color, let your breath guide you. Let your belly speak. Let your bones remember.

A journal is a space where your body gets a voice. Reflect not only on what happened today, but how it moved through you—what stirred, stretched, or softened. You are not just recording a past—you are sculpting a self.

These pages are your sacred canvas to FLIP old patterns, anchor presence, and awaken gratitude as your new baseline for power and joy.

"Acknowledging the good that you already have in your life is the foundation for all abundance."
~ Eckhard Tolle

Reflection

- **What is your understanding of gratitude?**
- **Where is that coming from? Who taught you this?**

"Acknowledging the good that you already have in your life is the foundation for all abundance."
~ Eckhard Tolle

"Acknowledging the good that you already have in your
life is the foundation for all abundance."
~ Eckhard Tolle

Explore Newtonian Gratitude

Look into your life and write down as many things as possible that you are grateful for, without overthinking it. Do it as a word cloud and write the things you already have in circles around the center cloud.

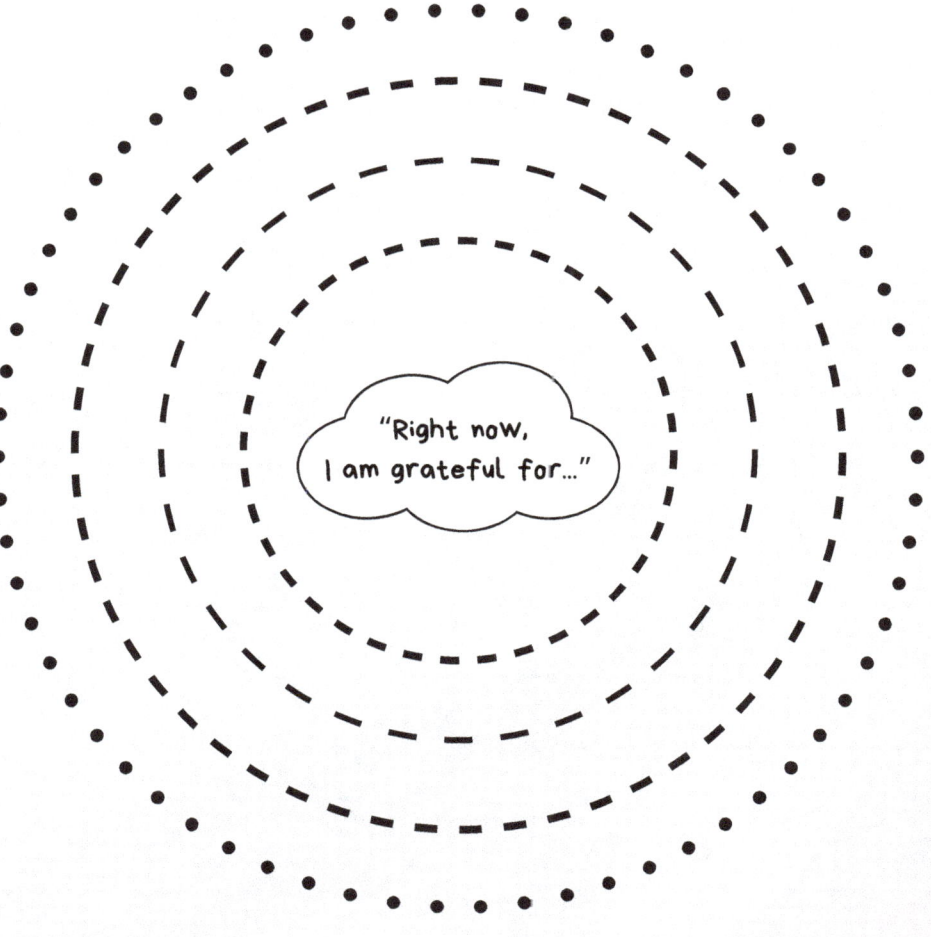

"Gratitude is riches. Complaint is poverty."
~ **Doris Day**

"Gratitude is riches. Complaint is poverty."
~ **Doris Day**

Somantic Awareness of Newtonian Gratitude

- How do you feel after writing down your cloud of things in your life that you feel grateful for right now?
- Sense into your body, where the gratitude sits. Mark the locations into the body's shape and write outside the shape some words that describe the romantic sensation of gratitude in your body!

"Feeling gratitude and not expressing it is like wrapping a present and not giving it."
~ William Arthur Ward

"Feeling gratitude and not expressing it is like wrapping
a present and not giving it."
~ William Arthur Ward

Explore Quantum Gratitude

Look into your **FUTURE** and write down as many things as possible that you desire to create, without overthinking it. Do it as an ocean looking toward the sunrise and write the things you imagine already having and **CHOOSE** to create the feeling of gratitude **NOW** as if all your desires were already fulfilled.

"I choose to feel grateful for..."

"What separates privilege from entitlement is gratitude."
~ Brene Brown

"What separates privilege from entitlement is
gratitude."
~ Brene Brown

Somantic Awareness of Quantum Gratitude

- How do you feel after writing down your cloud of **ANTICIPATED** things you **CHOOSE** to feel grateful for **NOW** before they even came to fruition?
- Sense into your body, where this deliberately created emotion of gratitude sits. Draw it into the body's shape all the locations and describe the romantic sensations of quantum gratitude in your body with a few words outside the shape!
- In what way does it feel different or the same as Newtonian gratitude?

"When you are grateful, fear disappears and abundance appears."
~ Anthony Robbins

"When you are grateful, fear disappears and abundance appears."
~ Anthony Robbins

100

# **2** Insights

- **Look at the previous 5 pages and contemplate:**
- **What have you learned about gratitude?**
- **What have you discovered about yourself?**

"Being thankful is not always experienced as a natural state of existence, we must work at it, akin to a type of strength training for the heart."
~ Larissa Gomez

"Being thankful is not always experienced as a natural state of existence, we must work at it, akin to a type of strength training for the heart."
~ Larissa Gomez

3 Intentions

- Big changes in the way we operate don't happen with one mental decision, rather with daily repetition that practises our new way of operation till our brain is rewired and instead of "new and unfamiliar" it becomes "normal and familiar".
- From reading the book chapter "FLIP - From Waiting to Creating" plus going through the creative exercises of this journal chapter, what do you INTEND to do with it?
- What daily - ideally 3 times morning, mid-day, evening with an alarm reminder - short practice - 1 to 3 minutes is enough! - will you do?

"If you concentrate on finding whatever is good in every situation, you will discover that your life will suddenly be filled with gratitude, a feeling that nurtures the soul."
~ Rabbi Harold Kushner

"If you concentrate on finding whatever is good in every situation, you will discover that your life will suddenly be filled with gratitude, a feeling that nurtures the soul."
~ Rabbi Harold Kushner

4 Vision and Commitment

Draw as symbols or figuratively your top three desired outcomes from implementing your intention into the visionary eye. Energize your vision with bright colors inside and around the eye!

"Gratitude is the ultimate form of receivership."
~ **Dr. Joe Dispenza**

"Gratitude is the ultimate form of receivership."
~ **Dr. Joe Dispenza**

Cyndee Paulson-Heer

Founder and CEO of The Sass n' Soul Life & The Sass n' Soul Network

http://www.cyndeepaulsonheer.com
https://thesassnsoullife.com/
https://www.instagram.com/cyndeepaulsonheer/
https://www.linkedin.com/in/cyndeepaulsonheer/
https://www.facebook.com/cyndee.paulsonheer/
https://www.instagram.com/the_sass_n_soul_life/
https://www.facebook.com/TheSassNSoulLife/

Cyndee Paulson-Heer is the founder of **The Sass n' Soul Life, Sass n' Soul Network**, and **Sass n' Soul Magazine**. Through these platforms, she helps women live authentically, lead with purpose, and live their legacy of impact. An award-winning writer and speaker, she combines personal narrative with practical tools to guide women in breaking free from unconscious patterns and charting lives of meaning and contribution.

Her most defining life moment came one quiet morning at her desk, coffee in hand and children nearby. While drafting a psychology essay on parenting, as the endless bickering of her two oldest filled the room, she suddenly saw how her unexamined patterns would become their "inheritance." Looking into her youngest son's big blue eyes, she recalls: *"I saw my children's future staring back at me. The awareness hit me like a stone dropped in still water, rippling out the truth: if I did not crack the code of my own life and model the person I wanted them to become, I would pass down my unconscious patterns like family heirlooms—and my past would become their future."*

Standing at that crossroads, she chose not to drift but to drive—and that decision became the foundation of her life's work.

Today, through books, journals, her magazine, and her vibrant Sass n' Soul community, Cyndee helps women discover their voice, align with their values, and live by conscious choice. She is currently expanding her reach with collaborative anthologies and the **Coffee Time with Cyndee** podcast—platforms that celebrate authentic stories, lifelong learning, and women leading with vision and volition.

Drift or Drive: The Guided Journal to Plan a Life You Love & Live It Out Loud

Welcome to Drift or Drive: The Guided Journal to Plan a Life You Love & Live It Out Loud

Every woman comes to a crossroads: will I drift through life, waiting for permission, or will I take the wheel and drive toward a life I truly love? This journal is here to help you choose the latter—to live boldly, bravely, and out loud.

These pages are more than paper. They are a safe space, a mirror, and a roadmap. Here, you'll find thought-provoking prompts, grounding exercises, and reflective practices to help you:

- **Clarify your values and purpose.**
- **Release burnout and approval-seeking.**
- **Redefine your story with courage and joy.**
- **Align your daily steps with the legacy you want to create.**

Some days you'll jot down a word. Other days you'll pour out your heart. Either way, each page you fill is a step toward becoming the woman you were always meant to be.

So here's your invitation: stop drifting. Start driving.
Because this isn't just journaling—it's you planning a life you love, and living it out loud, right now.
The pen is in your hand. The wheel is too. Let's begin.

Week 1: Compass (Values)

Your values are your inner compass. They point you toward a life that feels meaningful and personally fulfilling.

What are my top three values?

Where did these values come from—are they truly mine?

"When values are clear, decisions become easier."
– Roy E. Disney

Where do I live my values?

Where do I bend or avoid my values?

"When values are clear, decisions become easier."
– Roy E. Disney

Exercise: Make a "Values Check-In" chart. Write your top three values in one column. In the next column, write one way you're living each value. In the last column, write one adjustment you can make to bring more alignment.

Values	Ways you're living this value	Adjustment

"When values are clear, decisions become easier."
— Roy E. Disney

Week 2 – Map (Purpose)

Purpose is your map—it gives you direction and reminds you why you're on the journey.

I am here to _____.

What does purpose mean to me right now?

"The meaning of life is to find your gift. The purpose of life is to give it away."
– **Pablo Picasso**

If I weren't concerned with the expectations of others, what purpose would I choose to drive my life today?

Exercise: Write a short "Purpose Statement." Keep it to one or two sentences. Then place it somewhere visible (journal cover, phone wallpaper, mirror).

"The meaning of life is to find your gift. The purpose of life is to give it away."
– Pablo Picasso

Week 3 – Path (Contribution)

Your contribution is the path you leave behind—it's the impact your life makes on others.

My life contributes when I _____.

When my cup is full, what overflow do I naturally share?

"Your greatest contribution may not be something you do but someone you raise, inspire, or encourage."

What path am I carving that others might walk more easily?

Exercise: List three people (or communities) who are impacted when you live out loud. Next to each, write one small action you can take this week to invest in them.

"Your greatest contribution may not be something you do but someone you raise, inspire, or encourage."

Week 4 – Steps (Habits & Daily Choices)

The small, consistent steps you take every day create the bigger picture of your life.

What is one step I can take this week to align myself with my compass and map?

Where am I drifting or on autopilot?

"We are what we repeatedly do. Excellence, then, is not an act, but a habit."
– Aristotle

What is one micro-course correction I can make today?

Exercise: **Pick one habit you want to strengthen. Break it into a "Tiny Step." Example: instead of "exercise daily," start with "stretch for 5 minutes every morning." Track your consistency for one week.**

"We are what we repeatedly do. Excellence, then, is not an act, but a habit."
– Aristotle

✦ Optional Extra Week – Vision (Future Self) ✦

Sometimes the best way forward is to meet the future version of you.

If nothing held me back, what would my life look like 5 years from now?

"The future depends on what you do today."
– Mahatma Gandhi

How does my future self think, act, and choose differently from me today?

"The future depends on what you do today."
– Mahatma Gandhi

What would she thank me for starting now?

"The future depends on what you do today."
– Mahatma Gandhi

What single word or phrase captures the life I want to live out loud?

"The future depends on what you do today."
– Mahatma Gandhi

Exercise: Write a "Letter from Your Future Self." Imagine yourself 5 years ahead, living fully in alignment. Let her write back to you with encouragement, advice, and reminders of what matters most.

"The future depends on what you do today."
– Mahatma Gandhi

Kali Morris

Founder of Wealth IV Generations

https://www.linkedin.com/in/kholoud-morris-37bb05132/
https://www.facebook.com/kali.morris.2025/
https://www.instagram.com/kali.morris_wealth4generations/
https://kalimorris.mynewretirement.com/
https://kalimorris.com/

Kali Morris is a seasoned, state licensed, federally compliant financial professional, with years of experience in the financial services industry. Specializing in wealth accumulation, asset protection, and increasing net worth. Kali has a long track record of guiding clients to achieve their financial goals. Throughout her career she has demonstrated exceptional analytical skills and understanding of her clients' needs and wants. She believes that no one should work 40 to 50 years and not enjoy their hard-earned money. She made it her mission to get you to your perfect retirement destination by design.

Reflections:

Plan a Life You Love and Live It Out Loud

To you the real you: This book is a powerful reminder that creating a life full of purpose and joy starts with intention and action. Each story and insight shared by the coauthors encourages us to look inward, embrace our journey, and take steps toward a life we love. Use the tools to have create your own story the way you want it to be.

What's on your bucket list here are some:

- Locate where you are in your journey and be honest of how much you like or dislike and what you can control.
- Focus on all the great things that you are enjoying and blessed with (Kids, Health, Career you love, amazing partner ...)
- Observe yourself and mood and attitude what is impacting it, dehydration, not having enough financial safety, lack of organization, Identify your triggers.
- Take small and steady steps to change the norm and have new habits that will leave a legacy for generations to come.

You are not alone on this path
Kali Morris

Step 1 : Know where you are

TRACK YOUR MONEY

- **How much is my income? How much are my recurring expenses? what is my discretionary amount (left over)**

Plan A Life You Love and Live It Out Loud Now
A Bold Continuation of the Journey That Transformed Lives

- **Do I have debts? Do I have plans on how to pay them off? how much interest is it costing me?**

- **Do I have a budget? Do I Stick to it?**

Exercise: Write down your numbers for the last 3 months

Step 2: Stop the bleeding

PAYING OFF DEBT AND CONSOLIDATE

- **Do you know your interest rate on your debt? can you get it lowered? can you refinance? can you consolidate? can you transfer that debt to another lender with lower or no interest?**

Plan A Life You Love and Live It Out Loud Now
A Bold Continuation of the Journey That Transformed Lives

- **Do you have a plan to be debt free?**

Exercise: Call the lending companies and find out if you can get a better rate, activate notifications on your credit card when you exceed a certain limit.

Plan A Life You Love and Live It Out Loud Now
A Bold Continuation of the Journey That Transformed Lives

Step 3: Building for the Future

Starting an emergency funds and planning

* **Do you have a saving account? What is the interest rate your money is growing at?**

- **Do you know where you can save where your money can compound and grow faster?**

- **What was the last book you read about the basic of personal financial planning?**

Exercise:

- Decide a monthly amount to save in the right place to grow your cash value.
- Write down your financial goals for the next 5 years? how much you want in your bank account? in your saving?
- where do you want to travel to? what organization you want to support financially and with how much?

Plan A Life You Love and Live It Out Loud Now
A Bold Continuation of the Journey That Transformed Lives

Step 4: Create abundance

Evaluate and expand

- **How is new habit have been serving you? what do you need to adjust?**

- **What are the ones that kept you on track?**

- **What does abundance mean to you?**

- **What do you want to be remembered for?**

Plan A Life You Love and Live It Out Loud Now
A Bold Continuation of the Journey That Transformed Lives

Exercise: Write down what are your health goal? your relationship goals? how money can offer options and creativity to nurture and support you reaching your goals?

Plan A Life You Love and Live It Out Loud Now
A Bold Continuation of the Journey That Transformed Lives

Remember

- You are your own priority always.
- Maximize everyday
- You are in charge not your feelings.
- The decisions you make today will change your life tomorrow.

Self-Promise

"I am worthy of the beautiful life that I desire, and I will do whatever it takes that is legal ethical and moral to get there, I'll be brave and kind and loving and strong. and I will be remembered the way I want.

_____

Signature/ Date

Plan A Life You Love and Live It Out Loud Now
A Bold Continuation of the Journey That Transformed Lives

A Life You Love Continues...

Take a deep breath and celebrate.
You've done something extraordinary. You've dared to meet yourself on these pages, to face your dreams, your doubts, your fears, and your deepest desires. That is bravery. That is strength. That is you choosing *you*.

This journal was never just about filling in words. It was about awakening your voice, your vision, and your power. It was about releasing the need for approval, exchanging burnout for balance, and choosing faith over fear. Most of all, it was about remembering that your life isn't meant to be endured, it's meant to be designed, loved, and lived out loud.

As you step beyond these pages, remember: your story isn't finished. Every decision from here is a brushstroke in the masterpiece you're creating. Keep daring to dream with courage. Keep rebuilding with grace. Keep redefining beauty. The world doesn't need less of you, it needs the fullness of who you are, shining boldly, bravely, and unapologetically.

This isn't a closing chapter. It's the unfolding of your legacy.

With love and belief in you,
Hanna Olivas, The Resilience Maven™ | Author, Mother, Fighter, Creator of Sheconomy™

JOIN THE MOVEMENT!
#BAUW
Becoming An Unstoppable Woman
With She Rises Studios

She Rises Studios was founded by Hanna Olivas and Adriana Luna Carlos, the mother-daughter duo, in mid-2020 as they saw a need to help empower women worldwide. They are the podcast hosts of the *She Rises Studios Podcast* and Amazon best-selling authors and motivational speakers who travel the world. Hanna and Adriana are the movement creators of #BAUW - Becoming An Unstoppable Woman: The movement has been created to universally impact women of all ages, at whatever stage of life, to overcome insecurities, and adversities, and develop an unstoppable mindset. She Rises Studios educates, celebrates, and empowers women globally.

We Are

SHE RISES STUDIOS

A real-life community of women working to become the best version of themselves to change their lives and make the world a better place.

LEARN MORE

Looking to Join Us in our Next Anthology or Publish YOUR Own?

She Rises Studios Publishing offers full-service publishing, marketing, book tour, and campaign services. For more information, contact info@sherisesstudios.com

We are always looking for women who want to share their stories and expertise and feature their businesses on our podcasts, in our books, and in our magazines.

SEE WHAT WE DO

OUR PODCAST   **OUR BOOKS**   **OUR SERVICES**

Be featured in the Becoming An Unstoppable Woman magazine, published in 13 countries and sold in all major retailers. Get the visibility you need to LEVEL UP in your business!

Have your own TV show streamed across major platforms like Roku TV, Amazon Fire Stick, Apple TV and more!

Learn to leverage your expertise. Build your online presence and grow your audience with FENIX TV.
https://fenixtv.sherisesstudios.com/

Visit www.SheRisesStudios.com to see how YOU can join the #BAUW movement and help your community to achieve the UNSTOPPABLE mindset.

Have you checked out the *She Rises Studios Podcast?*

Find us on all MAJOR platforms: Spotify, IHeartRadio, Apple Podcasts, Google Podcasts, etc.

Looking to become a sponsor or build a partnership?

Email us at info@sherisesstudios.com